Are You Destined to Remain Friends?

Using the chart below, add up the number value of the letters of your name. If the sum is two or more digits long—for example, 23—add those numbers together (2 + 3 = 5) to get a single digit. You may need to do this again to get a single digit. This final one-digit figure is your magic number.

A = 1	J = 10	S = 19
B = 2	K = 11	T = 20
C = 3	L = 12	U = 21
D = 4	M = 13	V = 22
E = 5	N = 14	W = 23
F = 6	O = 15	X = 24
G = 7	P = 16	Y = 25
H = 8	Q = 17	Z = 26
I = 9	R = 18	

Now find the magic number for your BFF. Add her number to your number to come up with a single value. Reduce the number to a single digit as above if necessary.

This is your friendship factor. It reveals the future of your friendship.

What your friendship factor means

1 Your friendship is rock solid. It can't be broken apart by anyone or anything. You've won the lottery with this BFF!

2 Your friendship is pure magic. Like a pair of shoes or peanut butter and jelly, you work better together than apart. You complement each other, like blue and orange. This friendship is too strong to be divided!

3 Is there another friend in your inner circle? Of course there is! You've got so much love in your hearts it feels only natural to let other girls in. Sharing the fun doubles (or triples!) it.

4 A square has four straight sides. That makes it one of the most stable geometric shapes. Your friendship is just as stable. Don't forget to occasionally think outside the box—throwing a curve into your time together will keep this friendship rocking and rolling!

5 High five! This is the number of competition and victory. That sums up your friendship too. Sometimes you're up; sometimes you're down. Sometimes you fight; sometimes you're an unbeatable team! But in the end, you always figure out how to make your friendship a winner.

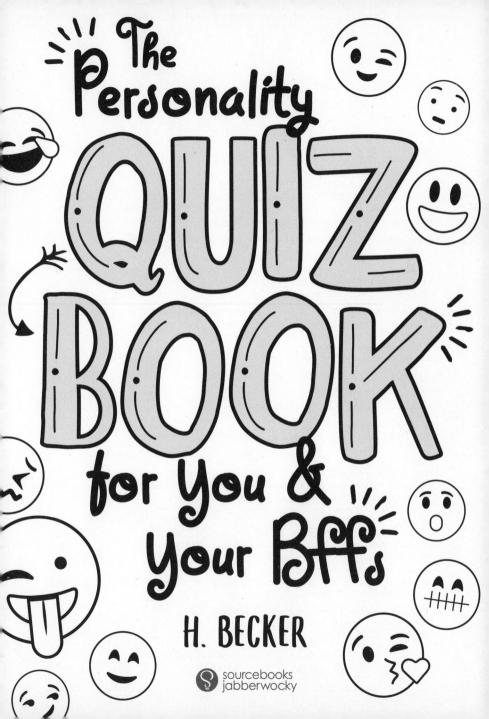

The Personality QUIZ BOOK for You & Your BFFs

H. BECKER

sourcebooks
jabberwocky

Copyright © 2014 by Helaine Becker
Cover and internal design © 2017 by Sourcebooks, Inc.
Cover design by Krista Joy Johnson
Cover images © ikopylov/VectorStock
Internal images © Michelle McAvoy/Sourcebooks, Freepik.com, Shutterstock/Viktoria Yams, Shutterstock/Natasha Pankina, Thinkstock/loliputa, iStock/Fafarumba, Shutterstock/Franzi, Thinkstock/Tris_White, Shutterstock/primiaou, Shutterstock/Alex Leo, Vectorstock/ikopylov

Published by Sourcebooks Jabberwocky, an imprint of Sourcebooks, Inc.
P.O. Box 4410, Naperville, Illinois 60567-4410
(630) 961-3900
Fax: (630) 961-2168
www.sourcebooks.com

Originally published as *The Quiz Book for BFFs 2* in 2014 in Canada by Scholastic Canada Ltd., an imprint of Scholastic Inc.

Library of Congress Cataloging-in-Publication Data

Names: Becker, Helaine, author.
Title: The personality quiz book for you and your BFFs : learn all about your
   friends! / H. Becker.
Other titles: Quiz book for BFFs 2
Description: Naperville, Illinois : Sourcebooks Jabberwocky, 2017. |
   "Originally published as The Quiz Book for BFFs 2 in 2014 in Canada by
   Scholastic Canada Ltd., an imprint of Scholastic Inc." | Includes
   bibliographical references and index. | Audience: Age 10. | Audience:
   Grade 4-6.
Identifiers: LCCN 2016058230 | (13 : alk. paper)
Subjects: LCSH: Typology (Psychology)--Juvenile literature. |
   Personality--Juvenile literature. | Best friends--Juvenile literature. |
   Children's questions and answers.
Classification: LCC BF698.3 .B4346 2017 | DDC 155.43/3--dc23 LC record available at https://lccn.loc.gov/2016058230

Source of Production: Versa Press, East Peoria, Illinois, USA
Date of Production: September 2017
Run Number: 5010513

Printed and bound in the United States of America.
VP 10 9 8 7 6 5 4 3

Table of Contents

6 You have so much in common! You think alike, act alike, even like the same clothes and music! But you don't always connect on a deeper level. Are you on parallel paths that never really meet?

7 Lucky number seven says your friendship is blessed by good fortune and a lifetime of fun. But don't take this friendship for granted. Luck can turn. It takes effort to make even the most favored friendships last. Beware of gossip. Jealous acquaintances can tear you apart.

8 Crazy eight defines your friendship. And your friendship is crazy all right! What do you two see in each other? You're as different as chalk and cheese, bologna and scissors! But that's what makes it work—that you bring different talents and tastes to the table. Somehow, this glorious, kooky friendship rises above your differences. Savor it though, because this wacky style of friendship doesn't always last. That doesn't mean it isn't a blast while you're in it though!

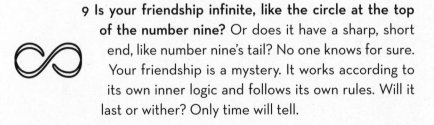

9 Is your friendship infinite, like the circle at the top of the number nine? Or does it have a sharp, short end, like number nine's tail? No one knows for sure. Your friendship is a mystery. It works according to its own inner logic and follows its own rules. Will it last or wither? Only time will tell.

How Well Do You Know Your BFF?

QUIZ A

Answer each of the following questions about your friend. Have her answer the same questions about you to find out your BFF IQ.

What does your BFF prefer:

1. Autumn or spring?

2. Sun or moon?

3. Unicorns or trolls?

4. Furry or silky?

5. New York or Paris?

6. Golden eagle or dove?

7. Tag or dodge ball?

8.   Wolverine or Iron Man?

9.   Mini golf or bowling?

10. Snowman or snow angel?

11. Candy corn or licorice?

12. Scrapbooking or beading?

13. 50-meter dash or 5K run?

14. Morning person or night owl?

15. Truth or dare?

SCORING

Find out which answers were right and give each other a point for each one. Your combined score tells you your BFF IQ.

How you rate

0-5 Go ahead—introduce yourselves to each other.

6-12 Delightfully different—and terrific together!

13-24 Can you read each other's minds?

25-30 Perfect partners in crime!

So You Think You Can Dance?

You don't have to be a disco diva to enjoy burning up the dance floor or to create your own signature dance with your BFF.

Grab your BFF and choose your fave tune. Start with some of these popular dance moves by following the diagrams. Then add your own personal flair for a sizzlin' routine that's yours and yours alone.

1. **The Grapevine.** This deliciously easy dance step will have you winding your way around the dance floor in no time. Mix it with a few other dance steps for extra punch. Then throw in some funky hand motions and shoulder shimmies. You'll have stirred up a juicy routine all your own! Each "step" has a number on it. The number indicates the order in which you move each foot.
   1) Move your right foot one step to the right.
   2) Cross your left foot behind your right foot.
   3) Right foot steps again!
   4) Left foot again, this time bringing it next to your right foot to complete one "grapevine." Continue in the same direction (until you run out of room); then,

switch feet and direction to groove your grapevine to the left.

2. **The Mambo.** Mambo is *the* classic Latin dance step—the foundation of salsa and many other fiesta faves. You'll be cooking with hot sauce when you show off this hot-and-spicy dance style.

Do this series of steps facing each other, so one partner is mirroring the other's steps. Or mix it up with other steps (like the Grapevine) for showstopping sizzle.

1) Move your left foot forward.

2) Shift your weight to the back foot.

3) Move your left foot back.

4) Pause with your feet together.

5) Move your right foot back.

6) Shift your weight to the front foot.

7) Move your right foot forward.

8) Pause with your feet together. Then go back to step 1 and start all over.

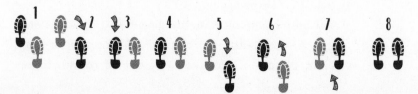

3. **Square Dance, Do-Si-Do.** Do this dance step facing each other. Circle around each other, passing each other on the right (so your right shoulders almost touch). Keep your body facing the same direction in which you started.

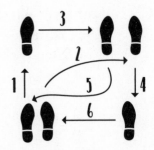

4. **Square Dance, Swing Your Partner.** Face each other. Link your right elbows and spin in a circle. Switch to link your left elbows. Spin in a circle in the opposite direction. Repeat as many times as desired.

5. **The Cancan.** Stand next to each other and do each step in unison.
   1) Jump in place, lifting your left knee.
   2) Land with both feet together, then kick your left toe in front of you as high as you can.
   3) Land feet together, then jump in place, lifting your right knee.
   4) Land feet together, then kick your right toe in front of you as high as you can. Repeat as many times as desired.

6. **The Macarena.** This party fave is extra fun when you do each step in unison with your peeps. To learn it, stand beside your BFF facing a mirror. Do each move first on the right side then on the left, holding for two beats on each side. Count the step numbers out loud and see if you can match each other's motions perfectly. Then do them in time

with your music! Invent your own dance by substituting steps of your own for a few of these.

1) Extend right arm out in front of you, palm down, then the left.

2) Turn right palm up, then the left.

3) Cross your right arm over your chest, then the left.

4) Bring your right hand to the back of your neck or head, then the left.

5) Bring your right hand to your left hip, then your left hand to your right hip.

6) Bring your right hand to your behind, then the left.

7) Swivel time! Bend your knees and rock your hips: left, right, left.

8) Jump and make a quarter turn to the right. Repeat from step 1 as many times as you like!

Will Your Friendship Last?

Answer yes or no to each of the following statements.

1. My friend and I are both blabbermouths—we can't keep secrets!

2. My friend and I share so many interests!

3. My friend has a selfish streak—she tends to put herself first.

4. I worry that my friend could turn on me.

5. My friend always knows the exact right thing to say to make me feel good about myself.

6. My friend is always nice, even when she's in a bad mood.

7. I get so jealous of my friend sometimes.

8. My friend always asks for my advice or to solve her problems for her.

9. My friend is 100 percent reliable, the kind of person I would trust to feed my fish when I'm on vacation.

10. My friend and I have one big thing in common. But other than that, we're as different as can be.

SCORING

1.	Yes 0	No 10
2.	Yes 10	No 5
3.	Yes 0	No 10
4.	Yes 0	No 5
5.	Yes 10	No 0
6.	Yes 10	No 0
7.	Yes 0	No 10
8.	Yes 0	No 5
9.	Yes 10	No 0
10.	Yes 0	No 10

How you rate

5-30 Enjoy the moment. Some friendships are for the long haul. Some are just for fun, just for now. You two may move on and go your own ways in the future, but that doesn't mean what you share now isn't special and wonderful.

35-55 Stick to it. Keeping a friendship strong requires plenty of work and plenty of patience and understanding. You two have the basics—trust, caring, and fun. Add a little elbow grease and this friendship might be one you will share for years to come.

60-90 Stuck like glue. There's so much good stuff between you—laughter, support, honesty, adventure. You encourage each other to be the best you each can be and truly celebrate one another's successes. That's the recipe for staying best friends forever. Give yourself a pat on the back and then give one to your BFF!

What Are Your Brains Made Of?

What's on your mind? What's on your BFF's? Divide up the brain pictured on the next page like a pie chart and mark what your brains are (mostly) made of! Here are some categories to consider. Add your own as needed!

- Clothes
- Schoolwork
- Pizza
- Video games
- World peace
- Crushes
- Social life
- Lunch
- Toe jam
- Conspiracy theories
- Kittens
- Planning a slumber party
- Friendship quizzes
- Zombies
- Music

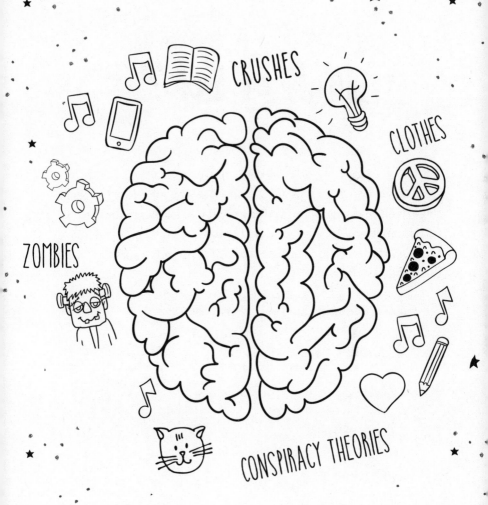

CRUSHES

CLOTHES

ZOMBIES

CONSPIRACY THEORIES

Meh or Eek?

Read over the items listed below. Are they ho-hum *checks fingernails and yawns* or do they send you running into the hills screaming? Answer meh or eek! for each item to get your scare score. Compare your scare score with your BFF's and see who's the bigger scaredy-cat!

1. A slug slithering across your bare skin

2. Spiders—big, hairy spiders

3. A rabid dog

4. Giving a speech

5. Camping—bears

6. Heights

7. The haunted house on the hill

8. An unidentified ooze rising in your basement

9. Hornets, hundreds of hornets

10. The zombie apocalypse

11. An alien invasion

12. Rats

13. Being trapped in a very small, dark space

14. Swimming in shark-infested waters

15. Walking through a cemetery at night

16. Piles and piles of homework

17. Skydiving

18. Leeches—the kind that can crawl out of the water to track down a meal

19. Taking a test you haven't studied for

20. A vampire in your bedroom, about to feast on your throat

SCORING

Give yourself one point for each eek!

How you rate

0-5 Ice runs through your veins

6-10 Cool as a cucumber

11-14 Nervous Nellie

15-20 Scaredy-cat

Which Trailblazer Is She?

Answer the following questions about your pal. Find out which famous trailblazer she most resembles and why!

1. **What motivates your BFF most?**
   a. Fame or power > Go to question 2.
   b. Adventure > Go to question 3.
   c. Curiosity > Go to question 4.
   d. Justice > Go to question 9.

2. **Which describes your BFF best?**
   a. A bit of a diva > Go to question 6.
   b. Determined and hardworking > Go to question 7.

3. **Your BFF is more...**
   a. Science oriented > Go to question 11.
   b. Artsy > Go to question 5.

4. **Which does your BFF prefer?**
   a. Nature > Go to question 8.
   b. Numbers > Go to question 11.

5. Your BFF prefers...

    a. Country life > She is GEORGIA O'KEEFFE.

    b. Social life > She is LUCY MAUD MONTGOMERY.

6. Which sounds more like your BFF?

    a. Fashion first > She is COCO CHANEL.

    b. Exploring new territory > Go to question 10.

    c. Fashion AND power, dahling > Go to question 12.

7. Your BFF is more...

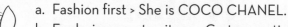

    a. Sporty > She is
       MISTY COPELAND.

    b. Literary > She is
       LUCY MAUD MONTGOMERY.

8. Which would your BFF prefer?

    a. Working with people > Go to question 9.

    b. Working with aliens > She is SALLY RIDE.

    c. Working with animals > She is JANE GOODALL.

9. Your BFF would rather be...

    a. In the thick of the action > She is HARRIET TUBMAN.

    b. The go-between, the communicator extraordinaire >
       She is SUSAN B. ANTHONY.

10. Your BFF is more...

    a. Adventurous >
       She is SACAGAWEA.

    b. Caring > She is
       FLORENCE NIGHTINGALE.

11. What does your BFF prefer?
a. Video games > She is KATHERINE JOHNSON.
b. Puzzles > She is HYPATIA.

12. Which country would your BFF prefer to visit?
a. Egypt > She is CLEOPATRA.
b. China > She is WU ZETIAN.

What your BFF's trailblazer persona means...

Sally Ride was the first American woman in space and was the youngest person ever in space. If your BFF is like Sally Ride, she is not afraid of new experiences. She likes to live on the edge and is often considered a leader. She knows how to be a team player too, and people like her. A lot.

Georgia O'Keeffe was an American artist whose distinctive painting style has made her an American icon. If your BFF is like Georgia O'Keeffe, she is an innovator and ahead of her time. She may have to overcome many obstacles to make her dreams come true, but a true visionary like her will always find success.

Coco Chanel was a pioneer in what we now think of as the modern fashion business. If your BFF is like Coco Chanel, she has exquisite style and a flawless fashion sense. She loves fashion magazines, fashion shows, and fashion trends. She'd like nothing more than to be a fashion designer herself!

Cleopatra was the last pharaoh of Egypt and a famous diplomat, strategist, and romantic heroine. If your BFF is like Cleopatra, she can literally rule the world. She has hidden strengths and a superb ability to read people and make them like her. She is also a very responsible caregiver and would make a great babysitter!

Jane Goodall is a British primate expert who has spent forty-five years studying chimpanzees in Africa. If your BFF is like Jane Goodall, she has a deep love of animals and people and a serious concern about the environment. She possesses great strength of character and a focused approach to life that will lead her to success.

Katherine Johnson was an American computer scientist at NASA. She contributed to twenty-six research reports, and her calculations helped ensure astronaut John Glenn launched and landed safely during the Friendship 7 mission. If your BFF is like

Katherine Johnson, she is good at math and science and has a very logical mind. She likes solving problems and creating new things. She is very tidy and orderly!

Hypatia was an ancient Greek philosopher, mathematician, and the first female astronomer. She was also the head of the famous School of Alexandria, where she taught the greatest intellectuals of the day. If your BFF is like Hypatia, she is a terrific teacher, with a sharp mind and an intuitive understanding for how to inspire others. She also knows how to wear a toga.

Susan B. Anthony was an American feminist and social activist. She was instrumental in the abolitionist and women's suffrage movements. If your BFF is like Susan B. Anthony, she is totally girl power! She will fight for what she believes is right and won't let anyone stand in her way.

Lucy Maud Montgomery was a Canadian novelist whose Anne of Green Gables book series is one of the best-loved stories of all time. If your BFF is like Lucy Maud Montgomery, she is creative and funny, with a mischievous streak. She is ambitious but not really comfortable with the limelight and would prefer to observe from the sidelines. She is very loyal to her friends and has incredible perseverance.

Sacagawea was a bilingual Native American of the Shoshone tribe who guided Lewis and Clark on their expedition to the Pacific Ocean and back, all while caring for her infant son! If your BFF is like Sacagawea, she is wise, courageous, and loves to travel. She is very interested in people and learning new things. She is the first to try new foods and fashions.

Florence Nightingale was responsible for founding the modern nursing profession. If your BFF is like Florence Nightingale, she has a sincere desire to help others. She is a logical thinker and very hands-on, a doer rather than a talker. She has so much energy!

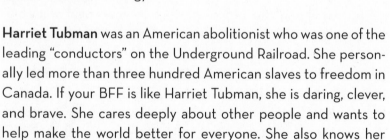

Harriet Tubman was an American abolitionist who was one of the leading "conductors" on the Underground Railroad. She personally led more than three hundred American slaves to freedom in Canada. If your BFF is like Harriet Tubman, she is daring, clever, and brave. She cares deeply about other people and wants to help make the world better for everyone. She also knows her own mind and is not easily influenced by others.

Misty Copeland began studying ballet at thirteen and became the first African American principal dancer in the American Ballet Theater. If your BFF is like Misty Copeland, she is strong, smart, and versatile. She can do anything she puts her mind to!

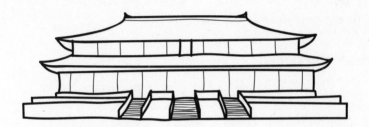

Wu Zetian was the only female Chinese emperor. Her reign was one of the most peaceful and culturally diverse periods in Chinese history. If your BFF is like Wu Zetian, she is definitely a leader! She is always exciting to be around but has a terrible temper. She is very trustworthy and loyal to people who deserve it.

Would You Rather...?

Which would you choose? Which would your BFF? Compare your answers to see how alike you are.

Would you rather...

1. get stuck without shoes or without toilet paper?

2. get a sunburn or frostbite?

3. spend one day in a viper pit or one night in a haunted house?

4. be sick with a horrible stomachache or look after a friend with a horrible stomachache?

5. not be able to read or not be able to write?

6. get trapped in a closet or accidentally locked out of the house?

7. eat bacon-flavored ice cream or
   super spicy chicken wings?

8. live without friends or live without money?

9. go hungry for a day or eat a fried mealworm?

10. have a week with tons of homework or a week with no
    homework but a big test on Friday?

11. get lice or athlete's foot?

12. go a day without talking or a day without food?

13. hold a poisonous scorpion or
    be chased by a ravenous tiger?

14. have more siblings or no siblings?

15. see into the future or be able to read minds?

16. face a horde of killer ants or a swarm of killer bees?

17. use a pogo stick on ice or a
    snowboard on slush?

18. be in the path
    of a tsunami
    or a lava eruption?

19. spend the rest of your life indoors or the rest of your life outdoors?

20. be seasick or lovesick?

SCORING

Give yourself a point for each answer you had in common.

How you rate

0–6 Rather be anywhere...but taking this quiz!

7–14 Rather similar...but you agree to disagree.

5–20 Rather freaky...how much you think alike!

Fill-in-the-Blanks Funny Story

Ask your friend to provide the pieces of information listed under each blank space. Do *not* read her the rest of the story. Your friend should give answers without any idea of what's going on in the story. Once you've filled out all the blanks, read the full story out loud! Want to swap roles? Find another funny story on page 74!

_____ woke up one morning feeling ill.
your BFF's name

She threw off the covers. Her feet were _____.
adjective

Her skin was _____. She had turned
adjective

into a _____! She got out of bed and
animal

_____ into the kitchen. Her family saw her,
verb ending in -ed

and they_____. " _____!"
animal noise ending in -ed   your BFF's name

they shouted. "You look _____!"
how your favorite food tastes

"Thank you," she said. Then she _____.

verb ending in -ed

At school, all the kids _____

verb ending in -ed

at her. They couldn't believe she had turned into

a _____. Suddenly she was the

same animal

most _____ kid in school! During

adjective

art class she was able to paint the most beautiful

painting with her _____. During

animal body part

phys. ed. she was the star at _____.

sport

In the cafeteria, she surprised everyone when

she ate with her _____. That's when

body part

_____ came in. _____

your principal   *your BFF*

was sooo _____! The principal

a feeling

said, "_____!" So _____

something a doctor says   *your BFF*

went home, crawling on her _____.

body part

She got into bed and _____

verb ending in -ed

herself to sleep. When she woke the next morning, she

looked down and was happy to see she was no longer a

_____. But when she went to brush her

<u>same animal</u>

teeth, she got another shock. Her nose had become a

_____!

<u>vegetable</u>

Do You See What I See?

Study this blob. Do you see an animal? Does your BFF?

SCORING

This activity is based on a famous test used in psychology experiments. It's called a Rorschach test and is used to assess people's personalities and emotional states.

What your answers reveal about your BFF and you

If you both chose yes...
- You and your BFF are quite normal. No, really. You are.

If you both chose no...
- Whoa! Are you sure you two are human? Or were your fathers androids and your mothers wildebeests? Do you each have six legs, perhaps? You two are so off-the-charts peculiar that the FBI has your faces on a poster that reads: Wanted—Identification of this species.

If one of you chose yes and the other chose no...
- You need to keep a careful eye on one another. *She* might turn into a cat before your very eyes. *She* might steal your socks. You know who we mean.

How Well Do You Know Your BFF?

QUIZ B

Answer each of the following questions about your friend, then have her answer the same questions about you.

Which does your BFF prefer:

1. Hoodie or cardigan?

2. T-shirt or turtleneck?

3. Miniskirt or yoga pants?

4. Bright colors or black?

5. Beret or baseball cap?

6. Trendy or classic?

7. Wild prints or sedate solids?

8. Mix or match?

9. Tights or knee-highs?

10. Heels or flats?

11. Bracelets or earrings?

12. Headband or ponytail?

13. Scarf or belt?

14. Classic or glam?

15. Vest or pullover?

SCORING

Add up your combined score—the total number of right answers—to find out your BFF IQ.

How you rate

0–5 Mix 'n' match. Your tastes in clothing may differ, but you agree your friendship is beautiful!

6–12 Sisters in stylin'. Your friendship will never go out of style.

13–24 Totally coordinated. Your friendship is ahead of the trend.

25–30 Matching outfits! You're perfectly paired, in all ways!

Princess, Peasant, or Jester?

So which of you is queen of the castle? And who's the dirty rascal? Take this quiz separately and then compare your answers to find out if you're a royal, a serf, or just plain silly.

1. **Which would you rather clean?**
    a. A toilet
    b. A diamond—a radioactive one
    c. A zoo enclosure

2. **Which would you rather have?**
    a. A ticket to a Broadway show
    b. A ticket to an NHL game
    c. A ticket to a comics convention

3. **Who would you rather meet?**
    a. Justin Bieber
    b. Duchess Kate
    c. Tigger

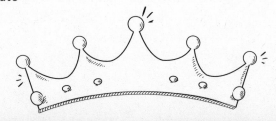

4. Where would you rather live?
   a. Disney World
   b. The Bahamas
   c. A cabin in the woods

5. How would you describe your pajamas?
   a. Pretty in pink
   b. Practical
   c. Printed with pictures of sushi

6. Suppertime! You're serving...
   a. Burgers and fries
   b. Sloppy joes
   c. Caviar

7. At school people consider you...
   a. A brain
   b. A pain
   c. Insane

8. What do you like to play?
   a. Four square
   b. Tag
   c. Capture the flag

9. Which animal do you like the best?
   a. Kittens are sooo cute!
   b. Puppies are sooo cute!
   c. Wildebeests are sooo cute!

10. Which is your favorite flower?
   a. Snapdragons
   b. Roses
   c. Tulips

SCORING

1. a1	b5	c10
2. a5	b1	c10
3. a1	b5	c10
4. a10	b5	c1
5. a5	b1	c10
6. a1	b10	c5
7. a5	b1	c10
8. a5	b1	c10
9. a5	b1	c10
10. a10	b5	c1

How you rate

10-49 Peasant. You're just an ordinary gal and proud of it!

50-70 Princess. Naturally you're royalty, dahling!

70+ Get yourself the jester's cap. You're clown to the court!

The Kookiest Contest

(For BFFs Only!)

There's nothing like a little friendly competition—especially when the contest ends up with two winners! Try the activities below. Decide together how you'll score whose efforts are "best" or "funniest."

1. Who can name the most Disney movies?

2. Who can cross her eyes best?

3. Who can name the most books that start with the letter *M*?

4. Who can list the most states?

5. Who can make the other person laugh first?

6. Who can throw a beanbag the farthest?

7. Who can write her name neatest?

8. Who can draw the best elephant?

9. Who can make the funniest sound?

10. Who can sing the highest note?

11. Who can take the silliest selfie?

12. Who can do the best Justin Bieber impression?

13. Who can scream the loudest?

14. Who can name the most superheroes?

15. Who can make the best monkey face?

What Sports Star Is She?

Being a sports superstar is not just about athletic talent. It's also about grit, determination, and style. Which sports hero is most like your BFF? Take this quiz to find out!

1. What is your BFF more likely to say?
   a. I have a need for speed. > Go to question 2.
   b. Slow and steady wins the race. > Go to question 3.

2. Your BFF is highly self-motivated.
   a. True > Go to question 4.
   b. False > Go to question 5.

3. Your BFF is happiest working...
   a. Alone > Go to question 6.
   b. In a group > Go to question 7.

4. Which term best describes your BFF?

    a. Focused > She is ALLYSON FELIX, Olympian in track and field.

    b. Versatile > She is SIMONE BILES, Olympic gymnast in vault, floor, *and* all-around.

5. Your BFF would prefer...

    a. A road trip > She is DANICA PATRICK, NASCAR driver.

    b. A sailing trip > She is MICHELLE WIE, professional golfer.

6. Which shape best represents your BFF?

    a. A straight line > She is SERENA WILLIAMS, tennis star.

    b. A circle > She is YUNA KIM, the 2010 Olympic figure skating champion.

7. Your BFF is more like...

    a. Summer > She is ABBY WAMBACH, Women's World Cup champion.

    b. Winter > She is IBTIHAJ MUHAMMAD, Olympic sabre fencer.

Who she is...

Allyson Felix. She's in the running for nicest person and best-est BFF ever! She has lots of determination. She will overcome anything that stands in her way. No one would ever call her a half-miler!

Simone Biles. Talk about versatile! Your BFF is good at everything! She's got a sharp mind too, and really knows how to land on her feet.

Danica Patrick. This gal has plenty of drive and ambition. When she puts the pedal to the metal, she leaves everyone else in the dust! But if she's not careful, she can run out of gas. Remind her to take some chill time to recharge her batteries.

Michelle Wie. She has an eagle eye and exceptional focus. Sometimes she gets distracted by her goals, but she will always stay the course, even when things get rough!

Serena Williams. When your BFF walks into a room, people notice. They love her and want to pay court to her! But she doesn't let it go to her head. She keeps her eye on the ball. She is also very open-minded.

Yuna Kim. She can figure out how to solve any problem, whether it's a homework question or what-to-wear crisis. With her upbeat attitude and winning smile, she makes everything look easy, but she's a hard worker. She also knows how to spin a story.

Abby Wambach. Hanging with your BFF is always such a kick. She knows how to have fun—give her a great idea and she'll run with it. She's a team player and a popular and effective leader.

Ibtihaj Muhammad. She's one cool customer—unflappable in a crisis and focused on her goals. She's always on point and never gives up!

Choose Her New Hairstyle

Is your friend looking for a new 'do? Help her figure out what her best look might be!

1. **She prefers...**
   a. Easy care > Go to question 2.
   b. Glam > Go to question 5.
   c. Funky > Go to question 10.
   d. Fun > Go to question 12.
   e. Everyone else's hair but her own > Go to question 17.

2. **Is she into sports?**
   a. Yes > Go to question 3.
   b. No > Go to question 4.

3. **Does she like to change her style now and then, or is one look good to go?**
   a. Change is good > She should try fun DOUBLE BUNS!
   b. One look is good > She should try SHORT AND SASSY!

4. Are her locks curly or straight?
    a. Curly > Add a HEADBAND to show off your natural curls while keeping them out of your face!
    b. Straight > Go for the CLASSIC PONY!
    c. Somewhere in between > Go to question 7.

5. Is her style sleek or sassy?
    a. Sleek > Go to question 6.
    b. Sassy > Go to question 9.

6. Is her hair long or short?
    a. Long > Go to question 7.
    b. Short > SIDE PART WITH GEL is the go-to 'do!

7. Cut it or keep it long?
    a. Get out the scissors! > Go to question 8.
    b. She'd never agree to a cut. > Try a FRENCH BRAID then!

8. Fashion forward or more of a classic type?
    a. Fashion forward > ASYMMETRICAL is the cut for her!
    b. Classic > A CHIN-LENGTH BOB is her go-to 'do.

9. Is she a girlie girl?
    a. Not at all > Give her SPIKES WITH GEL!
    b. Sort of > Leave it LONG AND FLOWY!
    c. Definitely > Go to question 16.

10.   Is she more artsy or more logical?
    a.   Artsy > Go to question 11.
    b.   Logical > Go to question 12.

11. Does she prefer dance or theater?
    a.   Dance > A TOP KNOT is the prima choice!
    b.   Theater > Go for big drama with
        wash-out HOT-PINK DYE.

12.   Is her hair curly, wavy, or straight?
    a.   Curly > Go to question 13.
    b.   Wavy > Go to question 14.
    c.   Straight > Go to question 15.

13.   Does she like to be the center of attention?
    a.   No way! > Let it grow LONG, LONGER, LONGEST!
    b.   You bet. > TWO POOFY PONYTAILS that look like
        teddy bear ears are super fun!

14.   Is her hair longer or shorter?
    a. Longer.> LOTS AND LOTS OF LITTLE BRAIDS are
        swingy fun for long-haired gals.
    b. Shorter > Make a zingy LIGHTNING
        BOLT PART and twist small sections
        of hair with multicolored hair bands
        for flashy fun.

15. Is her hair thicker or thinner?

    a. Thick and coarse > Go for a FAUX HAWK.

    b. Thick and shiny > Cut super short into a FUNKY BRUSH CUT.

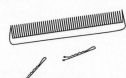

    c. Thin and silky > Shoulder length with BANGS is just the ticket!

16. Does she prefer shiny things or soft, cuddly things?

    a. Shiny things > Add fabulous jeweled hairpins and a cute TIARA!

    b. Soft, cuddly things > Use a bobby pin to add a VELVET BOW.

17. What would she like to change about her hair?

    a. Its color > Go to question 18.

    b. It's too curly > Get out the flat iron, then try a HALF PONYTAIL style.

    c. It's too thin > Get out the curling iron. A WAVY BOB is the answer.

    d. It just hangs there > Go to question 19.

18. Does she want lighter color, darker color, or different color?

    a. Lighter color > Try a LEMON JUICE RINSE for an all-natural Goldilocks look.

    b. Darker or redder > Try a HENNA rinse for a more exotic, French fashion.

    c. Different! > Go big or go home with PURPLE STREAKS!

19. Will she cut it?

a. Definitely > Go to question 20.

b. Nope > Go for a CROWN BRAID with some pretty or funky accessories, like fake flowers, to add flair.

20. How short?

a. Chin length > SIDE PART and let it SWING!

b. Super short! > SHAVE one side and let the top and back go all TOUSLED.

What each hairstyle says about your BFF

Asymmetrical cut. She's an independent, original thinker. And kooky—just a little kooky.

Bangs. She's sharp—a Powerpuff girl with bang-on style!

Chin-length bob. She enjoys sledding and is up for adventure!

Classic ponytail. She loves animals, especially sea horses and rocking horses. She enjoys vigorous activities like sports and mountain climbing. She loves country and western music and just horsing around with her friends.

Crown braid. She combines timeless elegance with a modern outlook. She knows how to make the best of a bad situation and turn life into a ball.

Double buns. She loves pastries. Sometimes she gets hot and cross, but she's always sweet at heart.

Faux hawk. She's super stylish and a total trendsetter. Everyone admires her fashion sense!

French braid. She has a very twisted sense of humor.

Funky brush cut. She's a no-nonsense gal and will win at the sweepstakes of life.

Half ponytail. She is cautious and doesn't like to jump into things. She thinks the cup is half-full.

Headband. This gal can fit in everywhere and adapt to new situations easily. Don't give her the cold shoulder!

Henna. No one ever called your brave pal chicken!

Hot-pink dye. She's a trendsetter and always cooler than cool!

Lemon juice rinse. Do blonds have more fun? If they are all like your BFF, they do. How do you bear it?

Lightning bolt part. Of course she's bright. She frequently changes her mind. She has a very sparkly personality.

Long and flowy. She's a true romantic and she adores her BFF!

Long, longer, longest! Whether she wears her hair straight, in braids, twists, curls, or locs, she isn't afraid to do things her own way or to tell others they should do them her way too!

Lots and lots of little braids. She's patient and has great attention to detail. She makes a great BFF because she remembers all your likes and dislikes!

Purple streaks. Can you say woo-hoo? This gal is a one-woman fun machine.

Shaved and tousled. With her lively and quirky personality, your BFF can make even bedhead look good.

Short and sassy. She's quick—good at math, sports, and problem-solving. She can do anything she sets her mind to.

Side part and swingy. She's playful and imaginative. She enjoys going to parks.

Side part with gel. She's very serious minded and determined to succeed. Will she? Of course!

Spikes with gel. Expect fireworks when this gal comes around! She's got strong opinions and isn't afraid to speak her mind.

Tiara. Diamonds are a girl's best friend, aren't they? And doesn't your BFF deserve them? Of course she does—she's warm, kind, and wonderful!

Top knot. She keeps everyone on their toes.

Two poofy ponytails. She loves to make others laugh. Why shouldn't they enjoy life as much as she does?

Velvet bow. She is a hopeless romantic. She sighs every time she sees a big-eyed puppy or a kitten. And unicorns! Oooh! She loves unicorns. She'd like nothing better than to wake up one morning in a historical novel like *Anne of Green Gables* or *Black Beauty*. She has beautiful handwriting.

Wavy bob. She has many moods, from classic to kooky. No wonder she's so exciting to be around!

Twins Separated at Birth?

Do you love the same things and think the same way, or are you and your BFF living proof that opposites attract? To find out, pick 1 for dislike or disagree, 2 for meh, or 3 for love or agree, for each item. Have your BFF do the same.

1. Fossils

2. Frozen yogurt

3. I am an excellent gymnast.

4. Maple-bacon cupcakes

5. Playing hangman

6. Lady Gaga

7. I'm an athlete.

8. Sunglasses

9. The Hunger Games trilogy

10. Funky barrettes

11. Skulls

12. Stuffed animals

13. I love to do experiments!

14. Romantic comedies

15. Hamsters

16. Skateboarding

17. Playing card games

18. I have a sensitive nose.

19. The smell of popcorn

20. Boys are silly.

21. Sci-fi movies

22. Purple stripes in your hair

23. Building snow forts

24. Dangly charms on bracelets

25. Adventure video games

26. I'm a thoughtful person.

27. Pancakes for dinner

28. I prefer being cold to being hot.

29. Chili peppers

30. I enjoy my own company and don't mind being alone.

31. Dolphins

32. Playing football

33. Santa hats

34. Stargazing

35. Anything cooking related

36. Jewelry making

37. Soup

38. Skirts

39. Chicken nuggets

40. Neon

41. I want to be a writer when I grow up.

42. Puzzles

43. Fishing

44. I can't sleep in an unmade bed.

45. T-shirts with cartoon characters on them

46. Making movies

47. I'd like a chinchilla as a pet.

48. I love math.

49. Square dancing

SCORING

Add up your answers that match. Double the total number—if you have 12 matching answers, for example, give yourself a score of 24 (12 x 2 = 24).

How you rate

90-100 Identical twins. You are so similar you might as well be clones.

50-89 Fraternal twins. You share so much in common, it's no wonder you're BFFs!

20-49 Soul sisters, maybe. Your differences complement each other; in fact, they're what make your friendship so strong!

0-19 Third cousins, once removed. You agree on one thing and one thing only: you love, love, love hanging out together!

Drawn Together

Do you two think alike? Do you *draw* alike?

On the next pages are some partially completed illustrations. Copy them twice, on two separate pieces of paper, one for you and one for your BFF. Then complete each picture. How similar are your finished pictures? How different are they? Whose are most realistic? Most colorful? Wackiest?

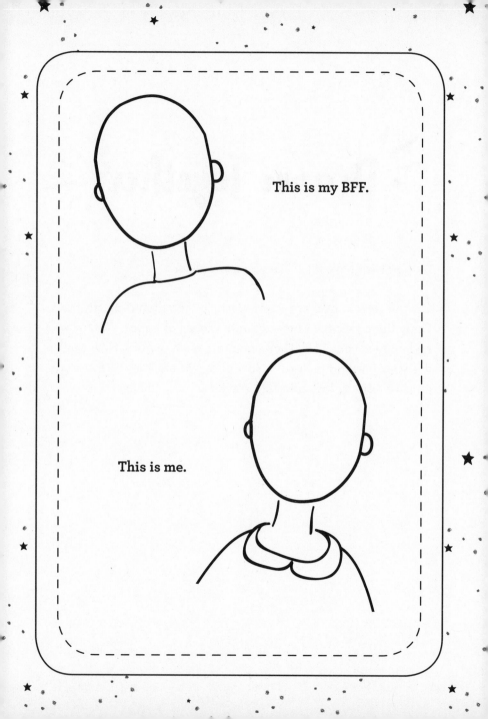

This is my BFF.

This is me.

Werewolf, Vampire, or Zombie?

So you're both far from normal. Everybody knows that. But are you truly monstrous? And if so, what kind of monster are you? And what is your BFF? Take this horrible quiz to discover the terrible truth.

1. **In the morning, you...**
   a. Take it slow but steady
   b. Are up and at 'em!
   c. Are so not a morning person—you're reaching for that snooze button!

2. **Which frightens you the most?**
   a. A zit. A really, really ugly zit.
   b. A bad hair day
   c. A fashion fiasco

3. **Choose a nail polish shade.**
   a. Apple Red
   b. Black Tornado
   c. Limeade

4. Which sport appeals to you most?
- a. Hang gliding
- b. Ultramarathon
- c. Touch football, in the mud

5. You have an art project to finish. What will you make?
- a. Something out of clay
- b. Something sparkly
- c. Something soft and fuzzy

6. Which would you rather do?
- a. A crossword puzzle
- b. Play Frisbee
- c. Dance

7. Choose a hat:
- a. Ball cap
- b. Beanie
- c. Wide-brimmed, glamour-girl sun hat

8. Do you sleep with a stuffed toy?
- a. No
- b. Yes, and it's old and falling apart
- c. Yes, and it's a soft, fluffy animal

9. Which would be your fantasy pet?
- a. A giant, pink gerbil
- b. A komodo dragon
- c. A unicorn

10. **Which is your fantasy vacay?**
   a. Paris, dahling
   a. Cabin in the woods
   a. Ahhh, spa

SCORING

	a	b	c
1.	a5	b10	c20
2.	a5	b10	c20
3.	a10	b20	c5
4.	a20	b10	c5
5.	a5	b20	c10
6.	a20	b10	c5
7.	a5	b10	c20
8.	a20	b5	c10
9.	a20	b5	c10
10.	a20	b10	c5

How you rate

50-95 Zombie. You care very little about what others think. You are very focused on your goals and not easily deterred from your path. You like to take things slow and are not much of a talker, but you really know how to get your point across.

100-150 Werewolf. You are very versatile. One day, you're creative and focused; the next, you're a whirlwind of activity. You love the great outdoors, animals, and jewelry with the moon and stars on it. You have a sharp mind and a very slobbery tongue.

155-200 Vampire. No wonder your friends come to you for advice—you seem older and wiser than most people your age. But you can sometimes be aloof, cold even. And who can blame you? You can be hurt by the smallest things: a harsh word, a sharpened stake. You have a tremendous thirst for knowledge.

Is She a Yogi? Are You?

Are you both human pretzels? Try these yoga moves to see if you're as flexible as a hair elastic or as stiff as a new note-book. Make sure you have plenty of space to move around, stay hydrated, and don't force your body into positions you're not comfortable with—yoga should be relaxing, not taxing!

1. **Cat-Cow:** Start by getting on all fours with your back flat. This is TABLE. Then arch your back, extending your neck and spine. This is COW. Round your back, rolling your shoulders toward your ears. This is CAT. Slowly alternate between CAT and COW to stretch your back. Ahhh... doesn't that feel great?

2.**Downward Dog:** From TABLE (see #1), straighten your legs, sending your hips as high as you can, and let your head drop between your arms. This is a terrific full-body stretch.

3. **Tree:** Stand with both feet together. Place the sole of one foot against the inside of the other leg, either above or below your knee (not on your knee). Hold your hands in front of you in the prayer position. Fix your eyes on a single point on the ground and balance on one foot for as long as you can. Then switch sides. This pose is great for balance and concentration.

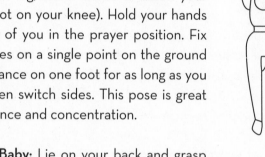

4. **Happy Baby:** Lie on your back and grasp both feet as shown, letting your knees flop out to the sides. Gently let yourself roll back and forth. Doesn't that feel good?

5. **Child's Pose:** Finish your yoga practice with CHILD'S POSE. Kneel on the floor with your knees slightly apart. Fold forward at the waist and rest your forehead on the floor in front of you. Stretch your arms out in front of you. Feel the amazing stretch in your back and shoulders. Ahhh...

Visual Puzzler

Sometimes two heads are better than one. Can you and your BFF solve these tricky rebus puzzles together?

1. OVER OVER

2. M1Y L1I1F1E

3. PROMISE

4. REST / YOUR

5. YOUR TIME

6. SGEG

7. GO IT IT IT IT

8. SEARCH AND

9. HI WAY / PASS

10. POUR

SCORING

Give yourself one point for each correct answer.

1. Over and over again
2. For once in my life
3. Broken promise
4. You're under arrest!
5. Your time is up!
6. Scrambled eggs
7. Go for it!
8. Search high and low
9. Highway overpass
10. Downpour

How you rate

0–1 Still at the starting line. But together, you're bound to cross the finish line of fun!

2–4 You are big thinkers. And big winners at friendship too!

5–7 There's so much fun in your friendship. And you two clever kids are bound to find it.

8–10 You're on top of the world. You two can solve any problem together!

How Well Do You Know Your BFF?

QUIZ C

Answer each of the following questions about your friend, then have her answer the same questions about you.

What does your BFF like best:

1. Eggs with ketchup or no ketchup?

2. Mild or extra spicy?

3. Sausage pizza or extra cheese?

4. Sushi or chicken?

5. Popcorn or tortilla chips?

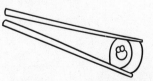

6. Dark chocolate or milk chocolate?

7. Almond or coconut?

8.   Oatmeal or puffed rice?

9.   Milk or juice?

10. White bread or whole wheat?

11. Tofu or turkey?

12. Stir-fry or stew?

13. Cantaloupe or honeydew?

14. Salty or sweet?

15. Cake or pie?

SCORING

Find out which answers were right and give each other a point for each one. Your combined score tells you your BFF IQ.

How you rate

0-5 Savory. You bring exotic tastes to your friendship table. Savor your differences!

6-12 Spicy. Like a pepperoni pizza, your friendship delivers exciting flavors and experiences.

13-24 Chewy. There's a lot to sink your teeth into in this healthy relationship!

25-30 Sweeeeet. You go together like fudge and brownie.

Fill-in-the-Blanks
Funny Story
(The Next Chapter)

Ask your friend to provide the pieces of information listed under each blank space. Do *not* read her the rest of the story. Your friend should give answers without any idea of what's going on in the story. Once you've filled out all the blanks, read the full story out loud!

_____ and _____ went
your BFF's name   a boy you know

up the _____ to fetch a pail of
a piece of furniture

_____. _____ fell
something gross   the boy

down and broke his _____. He started
funny object

to _____. _____ went
verb   your BFF

over to him and said, "_____."
something they say over the P.A. at school

_____ replied, "_____."
the boy   something your mother says

_____ got _____. She
　　　　your BFF　　　　　　　　　　　an emotion

_____ and _____
　　verb ending in -ed　　　　　　another verb ending in -ed

him. Then she threw the pail of _____
　　　　　　　　　　　　　　　　　　　　something gross

on him. "I never want to _____ you
　　　　　　　　　　　　　　　　　　verb

again!" she said. He said, "_____." So
　　　　　　　　　　　　　　　something you say to a pet

_____ went back down the
　　　　your BFF

_____, taking the pail with her. And
　　a piece of furniture

nobody ever saw or heard from _____
　　　　　　　　　　　　　　　　　　　　　the boy

ever again.

Best Friends 4-Evah Comic Strip

Your friendship is special, so immortalize it in your own comic strip! Draw yourself and your BFF in each of the frames below. Don't forget to add funny speech balloons and sound effects (BLAM! GACK!) Here are some ideas to get you started.

What she looks like when she's ready for bed.

Here's what we look like doing our own invented dance routine.

This is what we each looked like as babies.

Here's what we'll each look like when we are grown up.

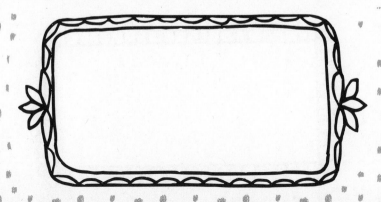

It was so hilarious when _____.

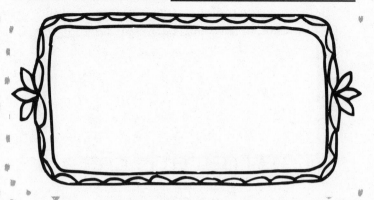

Oh no! BAD HAIR DAY!

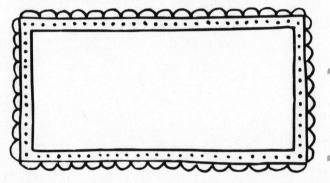

Here's what _____would look like as a zombie.

Here is us in our best Halloween costumes.

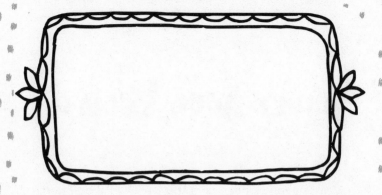

Here's what we'd both look like if we were our favorite foods.

Here's how we feel about dressing up in fancy clothes.

You're Sooo Weird!

Who's weirder, you or her? Take this very weird quiz separately and then compare your answers to find out!

1. **Which is most fun?**
   a. Eating worms—yum!
   b. Pretending to be a worm
   c. Having a worm as a pet

2. **Which word best describes you?**
   a. Interesting
   b. Funny
   c. Purple

3. **You swear there is WHAT living under your bed?**
   a. Dust bunnies—and they're alive!
   b. Monsters, naturally
   c. Cubic inches

4. When you were a little kid...

   a. You thought your stuffed animals were alive

   b. Your favorite stuffed animal went on playdates with you

   c. Your favorite stuffed animal organized your playdates

5. What color are your fingernails?

   a. Depends on the day. Sometimes they are pink, sometimes black, sometimes they have no particular color.

   b. Explain this word *fingernails*

   c. On our planet, we do not have fingernails; we have tentacles

6. If you were a tree...

   a. Your bark would be worse than your bite

   b. You'd drop seedpods on squirrels' heads just for fun

   c. You'd like to be a Christmas tree

7. Which kitchen tool is most like you?

   a. Knife, because you are sharp

   b. Can opener, because you are helpful

   c. Egg slicer, because you are an egg

8. You are putting together a volleyball team for the school intramural league. What team name do you suggest?

   a. The Volleywood Stars

   b. The Cheese Steaks

   c. The Volcano of Doom

9. Which practical joke is the funniest?
   a. Fake vomit
   b. The invisible dog on a leash
   c. The fake arrow through
      the head

10. Which fairy-tale character do you most resemble?
   a. Rapunzel, because she's hairy
   b. Cinderella, because she likes shoes
   c. Rumpelstiltskin, because he knows his own name too!

SCORING

1.	a5	b10	c1
2.	a1	b5	c10
3.	a5	b1	c10
4.	a1	b5	c10
5.	a1	b5	c10
6.	a5	b10	c1
7.	a5	b1	c10
8.	a5	b1	c10
9.	a1	b10	c5
10.	a10	b5	c1

How you rate

10-20 You are completely normal. Not weird at all. So not weird, in fact, that you are actually somewhat peculiar.

21-40 You are just the right amount of weird.

41-70 You are weirdly weird. So weird, in fact, that most other people think you are just pretending to be weird. But we know better.

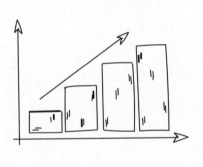

71+ You are off-the-charts weird. Run screaming to the hills weird. Your father is a lion and your mother smells like elderberries weird. Mad as a hatter, cuckoo as a clock, nutty as a peanut with a top hat and cane weird. The good news is there is a cure for your form of weirdness. The bad news is no one has discovered it yet.

What Type of Friend Are You?

Everybody has their own style of relating to others. Your temperament makes a difference when it comes to friendships too.

What's your friendship style?

1. **You tend to have...**
   a. Just one or two close friends
   b. Four or five gal pals
   c. Lots and lots of friends—the more the merrier!

2. **Your friendships tend to be...**
   a. Stormy
   b. Organized around common interests, like a sports team or fave activity
   c. Deep

3. **Which statement is most true of you?**
   a. You find it easy to make new friends
   b. Your friends change, it seems, with the seasons
   c. You find it hard to make new friends

4. Would you call yourself the jealous type?

    a. Yes

    b. No

5. How much do you share with your friends?

    a. Everything! They know everything about me and vice versa.

    b. Plenty—especially giggles and grins

    c. Not that much—I prefer to keep my feelings to myself

6. Do you worry a lot about what other people think of you?

    a. Yes! All the time.

    b. Sometimes

    c. No. Why bother? They'll think what they want to think.

7. Would you describe yourself as very sensitive and easily hurt?

    a. Who, me? Naaah.

    b. Sometimes

    c. Definitely

8. You've got to give a speech in front of a large group. Your BFF has offered to help you practice. What would you like her to do?

    a. Give me lots of reassurance and tell me I'm doing great!

    b. Help me correct my obvious mistakes, like when I'm talking too fast

    c. Nothing. I'd prefer to practice on my own, in private.

SCORING

1. a1	b5	c10
2. a5	b10	c8
3. a15	b8	c1
4. a5	b10	
5. a5	b10	c15
6. a5	b10	c15
7. a15	b10	c5
8. a8	b12	c15

How you rate

35–55 Shy. You find it difficult to break the ice with new people, but when you do, you are sensitive, loyal, and generous. The upside: the friendships you make will be real, deep, and long lasting. Watch out for: shying away. Give people a chance to know you by taking a risk and letting the real you show. You'll probably discover people are much more open and welcoming to you than you expect.

56–75 Intense. You care so deeply about people. Connecting with others can at times be exhausting and overwhelming. That's why you prefer to have one super close friend rather than lots of so-so friends, which can be great if you find that super special BFF to bond with and not so great if you don't. The upside: you're bound to have fabulous friendships! Watch out for: the jealousy bug. Don't forget to leave your BFF room to breathe. She'll love you all the more for giving her some space.

76-98 Easy-pleasy. People like hanging with you because, well, you're fun and easy to get along with. Not a lot of drama. The upside: you're popular and enjoy lots of varied friendships. Watch out for: Overextending yourself. You often find yourself pulled in several different directions, and you don't mean to let people down, but you're only one person! Try to be sensitive to other people's needs—they may not always be the same as your own.

99-105 Private. You might be the life of the party but find it tough to share your deepest feelings with others. The upside: you are very strong and self-reliant. You go, girl! Watch out for: burnout. No one can take on the world alone. Friends are for tough times as well as party time. When you open up and share your troubles, you'll find the load gets lighter and life looks brighter.

Extrovert, Introvert, or Ambivert?

Are you Little Miss Outgoing? Or are you more the shy, retiring type? Answer yes or no to find out whether you're a born extrovert (a person who is outgoing), introvert (a person who prefers their own company), or somewhere in the middle.

1. You like nothing better than a slumber party with lots of pals.

2. Too much noise wears you out.

3. The perfect day involves hanging out at home in your jammies.

4. You like quiet, on-your-own activities—reading, crafts, decorating your room.

5. You live for team sports.

6. Your favorite type of get-together is a sleepover with your bestie.

7. Your house is where all your pals gather—you love it when there's hustle and bustle!

8. You tell your best pals everything!

9. You're the one who makes social arrangements for your group of friends, making sure there's always something going on that you can do together.

10. You like to write in a journal or make drawings just for yourself.

11. Your favorite sports are ones you can do on your own, like swimming or running.

12. You feel most energized in a calm, quiet place.

13. You find it hard to focus when there are more than two or three people in the room.

14. Crowds—argh!!!

15. You're something of a performer—class clown, musician, or chatterbox.

SCORING

1.	yes 10	no 5
2.	yes 5	no 10
3.	yes 5	no 10
4.	yes 5	no 10
5.	yes 10	no 5
6.	yes 5	no 10
7.	yes 10	no 5
8.	yes 10	no 5
9.	yes 10	no 5
10.	yes 5	no 10
11.	yes 5	no 10
12.	yes 5	no 10
13.	yes 5	no 10
14.	yes 5	no 10
15.	yes 10	no 5

How you rate

75–100 Introvert. An introvert is a person who gets her energy from within. Your batteries are charged up when you are on your own and are depleted by large crowds, lots of noise, and commotion. This doesn't mean you aren't social—it just means you need lots of alone time to keep yourself feeling balanced and happy. You prefer smaller get-togethers with close friends to huge, noisy bashes, and solitary, creative activities to team sports. Because you are self-directed, you tend to be an original thinker and are not easily distracted by bells and whistles. As a result, you can achieve great success in many different fields that require intense concentration, especially the arts, sciences, and business.

105–120 Ambivert. Ambiverts are the most flexible personality type. You combine qualities of both your more outgoing friends and your more inward-looking ones, putting you in the "best of both worlds" category. You enjoy time on your own as much as you enjoy being "out there," and thrive on variety. Because you have qualities of both major personality types, you understand other people's feelings well. This makes you easy to get along with and a valued friend and colleague. Ambiverts do well in all fields, especially sales, education (you'd make a great teacher!), and collaborative fields like filmmaking or fashion.

125–150 Extrovert. An extrovert gets her energy from her interactions with other people. When you spend too much time alone, you get lethargic, bored, and even depressed. You shine, though, when surrounded by people. You love to be where the action is, and when nothing's going on, you're the one to get things started! Extroverts are natural entertainers, entrepreneurs, and politicians.

Two Heads Are Better than One

Working together, can you and your BFF figure out these brainteasers?

1. What do you have to give before you can break it?

2. What goes up but never comes down?

3. What loses its head every morning but gets it back again every night?

4. What has holes but can hold water?

5. What's as big as an elephant but weighs nothing?

6. What five-letter word becomes shorter when you add two letters to it?

7. Without it, I'm dead. If I'm not, then I'm behind. What am I?

8. What can be cracked, made, told, and played?

9. The more you take of me, the more you leave behind. What am I?

10. What has eyes but cannot see?

11. Mary's father has four children; three are named Nana, Nene, and Nini. What is the fourth child's name?

12. It lives without a body, hears without ears, speaks without a mouth, and is born in air. What is it?

13. What goes around and around the wood but never goes into the wood?

14. What do you break every time you name it?

15. What has four fingers and one thumb but is not alive?

16. How many letters are in the alphabet?

17. You can draw me, fire me, or fill me in. What am I?

18. Where do you find roads without vehicles, forests without trees, and cities without houses?

19. How many seconds are there in a year?

20. There's a one-story house that's all yellow inside. The floor is yellow, the lamps are yellow, the walls are yellow—everything is yellow. So what color are the interior stairs?

SCORING

Add up your combined score—the total number of right answers—to find out how you rate.

1. Your word
2. Your age
3. A pillow
4. A sponge
5. An elephant's shadow
6. Short
7. A head
8. A joke
9. Footsteps
10. A potato
11. Mary
12. An echo
13. The bark on a tree
14. Silence
15. A glove
16. Eleven! Count them: THE ALPHABET
17. A blank
18. On a map
19. Twelve: January 2nd, February 2nd, etc.
20. There are no stairs. The house is only one story.

How you rate

0-5 Riddle newbies. Luckily you're clever at choosing friends!

6-10 Sisters in solvin'. Your friendship is a smart idea!

11-14 Both brill! Great minds think alike!

15-20 Pure genius! You're a pair of prodigies and an A+ team!

Cat or Dog?

Are you a cat person or a dog person? What about your BFF? Take this quiz to find out whether you are purrfectly matched or doggone different!

1. **Which would you prefer?**
   a. Playing catch with a Frisbee
   b. Snoozing on top of a radiator
   c. Taking a walk in the woods

2. **Would you call yourself a people person?**
   a. Yes. Definitely.
   b. Sometimes. I can be outgoing, but I also value alone time.
   c. Not so much. People consider me a very private person.

3. **Which sport do you prefer?**
   a. Yoga
   b. Track and field
   c. Fishing

4. It's your birthday. What's your dream day?

    a. Spa, dahling

    b. Hanging out at home

    c. Rambling through a city with my
       bestie, taking in all the sights and sounds

5. You're cooking dinner! What's on the menu?

    a. Barbecued salmon

    b. Barbecued baby back ribs

    c. Veggie pizza

6. Your bestie has given you a new nickname. What is it?

    a. Scooby

    b. Garfield

    c. Cuddles McGee

7. Is the glass half-empty or half-full?

    a. Half-full

    b. Full, silly!

    c. Empty, but who cares as long as the glass is crystal!

8. Which do you prefer?

    a. Fries with ketchup

    b. Fries with nacho cheese

    c. Fries with chili

9. You are buying a gift for your bestie. What will it be?

    a. A soccer ball

    b. A fluffy stuffed animal

    c. A can of tuna

10. What animal drives you crazy?
   a. Evil mice. Definitely. Evil. Mice.
   b. Did someone say squirrel?
   c. That annoying bird that starts tweeting before dawn.

SCORING

1. a1	b3	c5
2. a1	b3	c5
3. a3	b1	c5
4. a5	b3	c1
5. a5	b1	c3
6. a1	b5	c3
7. a3	b1	c5
8. a5	b1	c3
9. a3	b1	c5
10. a5	b1	c3

10-22 100% Dog person. You are affectionate, eager to please, and open-minded. You also have a tendency to slobber and jump up on people. But that doesn't stop them from loving you for your joyful enthusiasm, playful spirit, and floppy ears. You are good at following instructions and an excellent team player.

23-36 Cat-dog combo. You are so lucky—a versatile person who combines the best quality of both dogs and cats in one special package! "Cogs" like you have beautiful hair and, naturally, superior grooming skills. You've got plenty of self-confidence and nothing gets you down.

37-50 100% Cat person. You are a rare breed—independent, brilliant, and capable. You are definitely a leader, not a follower. Graceful, tidy, and prone to hairballs, you win the admiration of all you meet. You bounce back from adversity—perhaps you really do have nine lives! Avoid people named Tweety or Jerry—they are out to get you.

What's Your EQ?

You've probably heard of IQ tests. They're supposed to measure intelligence. EQ tests measure emotional smarts—how good you are at recognizing and responding to emotions.

How well do you know your own feelings? What about your BFF's? Take this quiz to find out if you are emotionally aware or emotionally AWOL.

1. **You usually hang out with the same group of gal pals. Do you always know exactly how each person in your clique feels about each other?**
   a. Yes. I know all about who's tighter than tight and who are rivals.
   b. Sometimes. People's feelings can change awfully fast!
   c. Yes. We're all super good friends. Why else would we hang out together?

2. **You woke up this morning feeling unsettled and unhappy. Do you know why?**
   a. Must have woken up on the wrong side of the bed.
   b. Maybe because I had a bad dream?
   c. Yes. It was because of the argument I had with my sister before we went to sleep.

3. **True or false: When you make a mistake, you get really down on yourself and become super self-critical.**

   a. Totally
   b. Sometimes
   c. No way! Everyone makes mistakes now and then. Let it go.

4. **You have to go see your teacher about your bad grade on an English test. How does this make you feel?**

   a. Uncomfortable, but you take a deep breath and get it over with
   b. Not great, but you know she will help you figure out how to improve your work, so it will work out in the end
   c. Anxious and unhappy—you hate being put on the spot

5. **Do people call you a drama queen because you tend to overreact to little things?**
   a. Nope
   b. Sometimes
   c. Omigod, that is soooo me!

6. Would you describe yourself as a good judge of character?

    a. Yes, I can often tell if someone is truly kind and honest or if they are putting on an act

    b. Usually, although it surprises me when someone turns out to be more of a "frenemy" than a friend

    c. I always thought so, but lately I get confused by people who say one thing and do another

7. You're arguing with your brother about whose turn it is to wash the dishes. Things are starting to get pretty heated and out of control. What do you do?

    a. Suggest you both cool down a bit before making a decision

    b. Scream at him and call him names

    c. Just go ahead and do the dishes—even though you know it's his turn

8. You have the chance to play on a Select soccer team. You know it will require a huge time commitment, and you're not sure if you are ready to do that. How will you make your decision?

    a. Listen to your gut and follow your instincts

    b. Let your coach or your parents decide

    c. Make a list of pros and cons to help you decide

9. Which statement best describes you?
   a. I make friends easily
   b. I get along well with others, but I need plenty of time before I let others get close to me
   c. I sometimes find it difficult to get to know other people

10. Your bestie's pet died. She feels terrible. What do you do?
   a. Convince her to go out and have some fun to take her mind off Fluffy
   b. Let her cry and express your sympathy. Sometimes people just need to let their feelings out.
   c. Give her some time to herself. No one wants people around at a time like this, do they?

SCORING

1. a3	b2	c1
2. a1	b2	c3
3. a1	b2	c3
4. a3	b2	c1
5. a3	b2	c1
6. a3	b2	c1
7. a3	b1	c2
8. a3	b1	c2
9. a3	b2	c1
10. a2	b3	c1

How you rate

10–16 Fair. You and your classmates are all going through lots of changes now. That makes it hard to keep on top of your own feelings and motivations, let alone figure out what's going on inside other people! You can develop your EQ by allowing yourself some quiet time to listen to your intuition. Spend some time observing others carefully too. You can learn a lot about what's going on inside other people by watching their facial expressions and body language. Before long, you will be a whiz at understanding yourself and others!

17-23 Good. You have a solid understanding of what makes you tick and what gets under your skin. You have good self-control too, and you don't let yourself fly off the handle or sink into a funk at every little thing. You also are pretty good at reading other people and can behave in ways that help you all get along. Continue developing your EQ to build even better friendships and healthier self-awareness.

24-30 Excellent. You are a pro at understanding human nature and human behavior. You have a high degree of self-knowledge, and that gives you plenty of self-confidence. Others respect you, and you, in turn, respect them—perhaps because you recognize their feelings and respond sensitively and appropriately. Remember that your classmates may not all be as emotionally intelligent as you are—don't forget to cut them some slack. They'll appreciate learning from your wise and caring example.